Published 2006
by firsthouse music books
a division of firsthouse music publishing

firsthouse music publications
86 Taplings Rd
Winchester Hants SO22 6HF
United Kingdom

firsthouse music publishing
I have had holidays in

London   Paris   New York

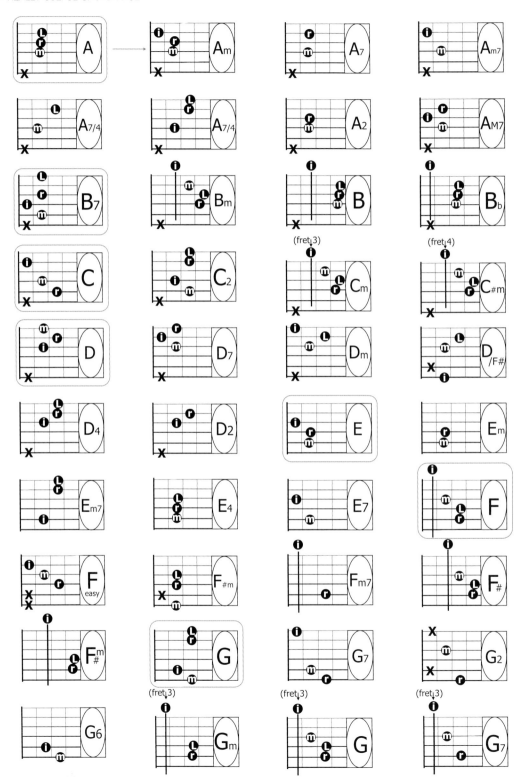

SCHOOL OF ROCK

HOW TO TUNE A BASS GUITAR

WITHOUT A TUNER

1 Identify the bass guitar notes

E

A

D

G

If you're playing a standard bass guitar, you will notice that your bass has only 4 strings. The standard tuning for a 4 string bass is **E, A, D, G** (the same as the four lowest strings on the guitar but one octave lower). The bass strings are tuned in 1

protected by reCAPTCHA

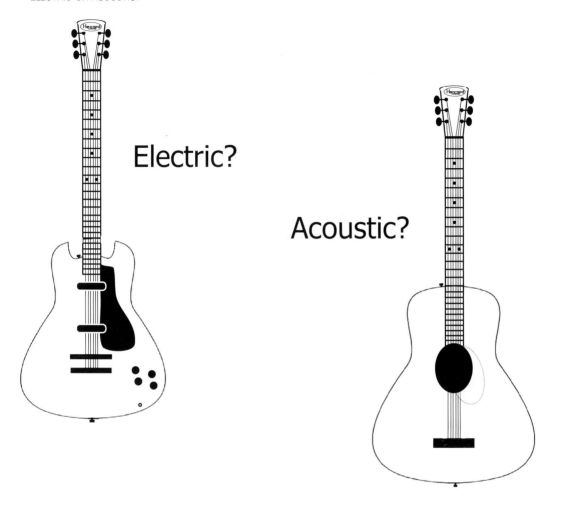

Electric?

Acoustic?

This book is perfect for both!

t has been written and designed to teach you the best possible foundations
for general guitar playing whatever the style of music or type of guitar.
By learning the skills and techniques in this book, you will be very well
equipped to specialize later on as you progress and develop into the
best guitarist you can be!

All teaching methods in this course book © andy read
andy@guitarsteps.com

firsthouse music publishing
www.guitarsteps.com

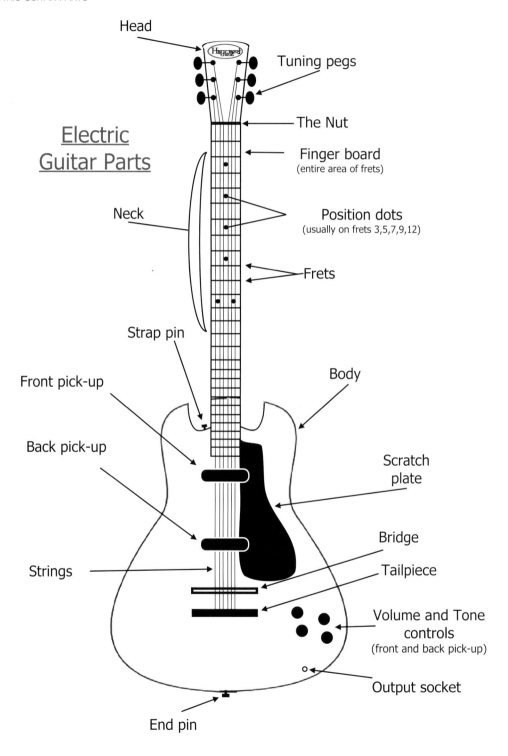

Electric
Guitar Parts

Head

Tuning pegs

The Nut

Finger board
(entire area of frets)

Neck

Position dots
(usually on frets 3,5,7,9,12)

Frets

Strap pin

Body

Front pick-up

Back pick-up

Scratch
plate

Bridge

Strings

Tailpiece

Volume and Tone
controls
(front and back pick-up)

Output socket

End pin

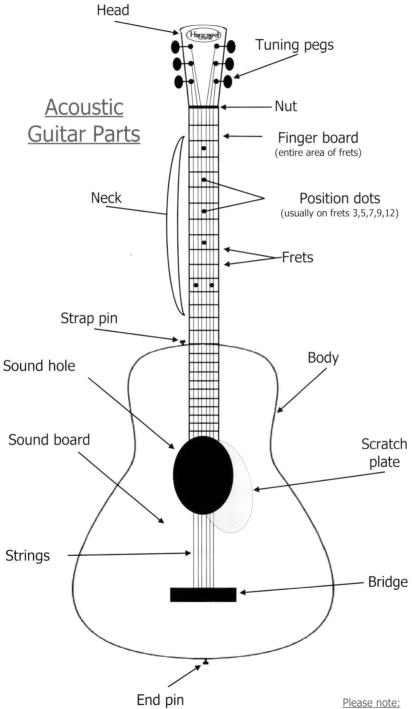

Head

Tuning pegs

Acoustic
Guitar Parts

Nut

Finger board
(entire area of frets)

Neck

Position dots
(usually on frets 3,5,7,9,12)

Frets

Strap pin

Sound hole

Body

Sound board

Scratch
plate

Strings

Bridge

End pin

Please note:
Both diagrams show general guitar parts.
Not every guitar will have every part shown.

contents

welcome! • practice • finger names • tuning the guitar • reading the chords • speed tests • target times.

Welcome!

The purpose of this book is quite simple. It sets out to teach you how to play the guitar. Every teacher will teach in different styles, and no student will learn in exactly the same ways, but trying to make everything as easy to understand as possible has always been my first priority!

When I started to learn the guitar many years ago, I remember standing in a guitar shop looking through the beginner books. I got so excited and enthusiastic about the first 3 pages, and then found it very difficult to understand anything from page 4 onwards! Years later as I studied teaching as a career, and eventually taught in primary schools, I began to understand the importance of learning in small steps.

Every great journey always starts with that one small step. And then another - and another, etc. It is my aim to inspire you to tackle these steps at your own pace, and in your own time, and little by little, step by step, you will see how much you can achieve!

I've tried to lay out the book in a user-friendly way. There are some things you don't need to know about right now that will only add to any confusion, and might discourage you as you suddenly realise how far you still have to go!

Remember this is a book with limitations written for beginners and people who want a refresher course. There are many books out there that offer 1001 technical and more advanced guitar and musical theories. If the information in these pages help and encourage you in a few more steps of your playing journey - it's been worth it!

Practice

The key to progress is playing a little, often. You have to get across to your fingers that things are going to be different from now on, and the aching and soreness is just part of that process! It won't last for long, but it is a sign you are doing something good! Don't feel you have to become a star overnight. Focus on getting a routine into your life. Give it four weeks to begin with. Decide on what time of day suits you, and how many minutes you can practice each day, and then try and stick to it.

For four weeks.

If you can hit 10 minutes, 4/5 times a week, I promise you will see something happening in that month!

Finger names

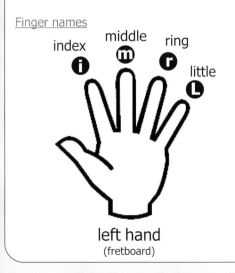

left hand
(fretboard)

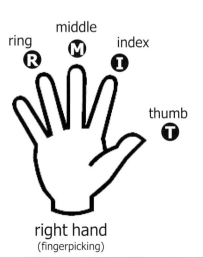

right hand
(fingerpicking)

Tuning the guitar

Your guitar needs to be in tune before you are going to get any good sounds from it. The only trouble is that tuning is an art in itself, and something else that you have to learn to get better at. My advice for all my students is this: get a good electronic tuner! (KORG GA-30 £15ish) You have the rest of your life to train your ears for perfect pitch, but you need to learn quickly now, and today's technology gives us these effective low cost machines.

Reading the chords

People display chord diagrams in different ways, but whichever way you learn from first, you will quickly get used to it.

I have made the size of the strings quite plain to see, and if you always remember <u>the thick string is first from your face,</u> (when you have the guitar in your normal playing position) you won't go far wrong.

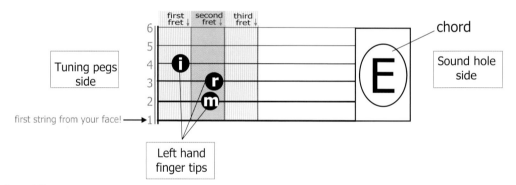

Speed Tests

Remember; it's not about you comparing yourself to someone else, but about <u>you</u> getting better compared with last week!

I use target times and speed tests in my teaching because it shows students just how well they are progressing. It's not about speed, but it is about finding out how long it takes you to do an exercise as smoothly and cleanly as possible. After a week's practice, you find out that you still play that exercise well, but it takes 20 seconds less time. That's progress!

Target Time and Beginner's Average Time (BAT)

TT: 30-40s:

means that the Target Time you should be aiming at for that step is between 30 and 40 seconds.
BAT:1.00-1.30:

means that the Beginner's Average Time is (usually) between one minute, and one minute thirty seconds.

HOW TO TUNE A BASS GUITAR

WITHOUT A TUNER

SCHOOL OF ROCK

1

Identify the bass guitar notes

E A D G

If you're playing a standard bass guitar, you will notice that your bass has only 4 strings. The standard tuning for a 4 string bass is **E**, **A**, **D**, **G** (the same as the four lowest strings on the guitar but one octave lower). The bass strings are tuned in t

protected by reCAPTCHA

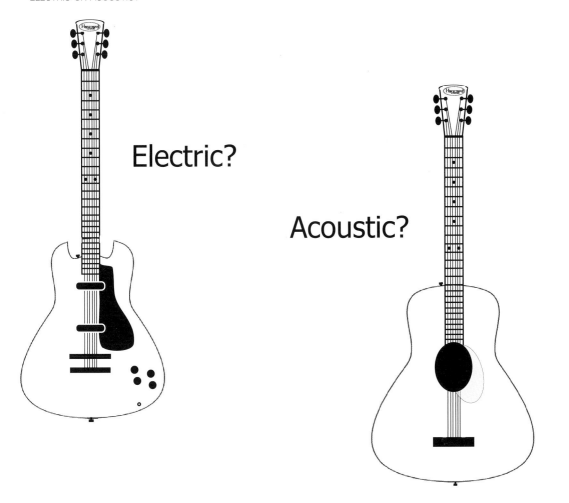

Electric?

Acoustic?

This book is perfect for both!

t has been written and designed to teach you the best possible foundations for general guitar playing whatever the style of music or type of guitar. By learning the skills and techniques in this book, you will be very well equipped to specialize later on as you progress and develop into the best guitarist you can be!

All teaching methods in this course book © andy read
andy@guitarsteps.com

firsthouse music publishing
Copyright © Andy Read 2006
www.guitarsteps.com

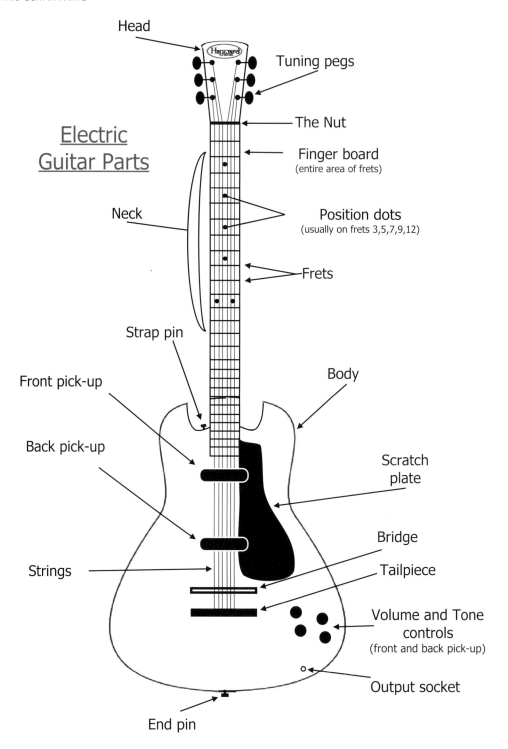

Electric Guitar Parts

Head

Tuning pegs

The Nut

Finger board
(entire area of frets)

Position dots
(usually on frets 3,5,7,9,12)

Neck

Frets

Strap pin

Body

Front pick-up

Back pick-up

Scratch plate

Bridge

Strings

Tailpiece

Volume and Tone controls
(front and back pick-up)

Output socket

End pin

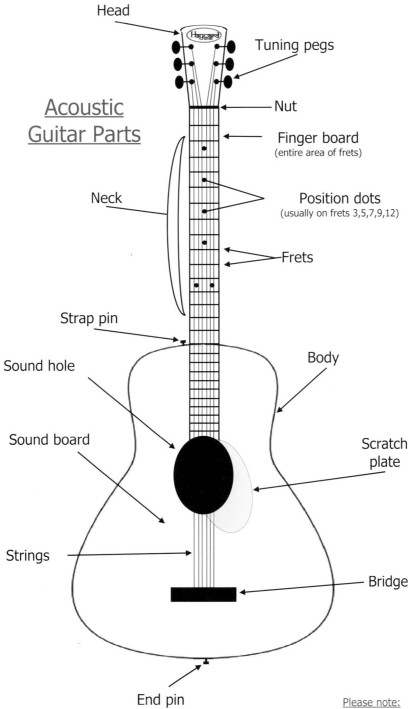

Head

Tuning pegs

Acoustic
Guitar Parts

Nut

Finger board
(entire area of frets)

Neck

Position dots
(usually on frets 3,5,7,9,12)

Frets

Strap pin

Sound hole

Body

Sound board

Scratch
plate

Strings

Bridge

End pin

contents

welcome! • practice • finger names • tuning the guitar • reading the chords • speed tests • target times.

Welcome!

The purpose of this book is quite simple. It sets out to teach you how to play the guitar. Every teacher will teach in different styles, and no student will learn in exactly the same ways, but trying to make everything as easy to understand as possible has always been my first priority!

When I started to learn the guitar many years ago, I remember standing in a guitar shop looking through the beginner books. I got so excited and enthusiastic about the first 3 pages, and then found it very difficult to understand anything from page 4 onwards! Years later as I studied teaching as a career, and eventually taught in primary schools, I began to understand the importance of learning in small steps.

Every great journey always starts with that one small step. And then another - and another, etc. It is my aim to inspire you to tackle these steps at your own pace, and in your own time, and little by little, step by step, you will see how much you can achieve!

I've tried to lay out the book in a user-friendly way. There are some things you don't need to know about right now that will only add to any confusion, and might discourage you as you suddenly realise how far you still have to go!

Remember this is a book with limitations written for beginners and people who want a refresher course. There are many books out there that offer 1001 technical and more advanced guitar and musical theories. If the information in these pages help and encourage you in a few more steps of your playing journey - it's been worth it!

Practice

The key to progress is playing a little, often. You have to get across to your fingers that things are going to be different from now on, and the aching and soreness is just part of that process! It won't last for long, but it is a sign you are doing something good! Don't feel you have to become a star overnight. Focus on getting a routine into your life. Give it four weeks to begin with. Decide on what time of day suits you, and how many minutes you can practice each day, and then try and stick to it.

For four weeks.

If you can hit 10 minutes, 4/5 times a week, I promise you will see something happening in that month!

Finger names

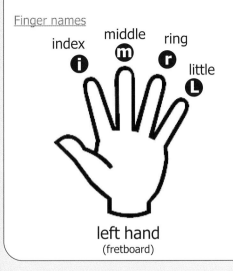

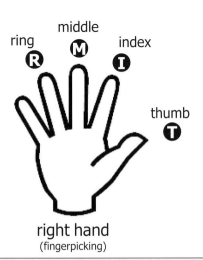

Tuning the guitar

Your guitar needs to be in tune before you are going to get any good sounds from it. The only trouble is that tuning is an art in itself, and something else that you have to learn to get better at. My advice for all my students is this: get a good electronic tuner! (KORG GA-30 £15ish) You have the rest of your life to train your ears for perfect pitch, but you need to learn quickly now, and today's technology gives us these effective low cost machines.

first string from your face!

Reading the chords

People display chord diagrams in different ways, but whichever way you learn from first, you will quickly get used to it.

I have made the size of the strings quite plain to see, and if you always remember <u>the thick string is first from your face,</u> (when you have the guitar in your normal playing position) you won't go far wrong.

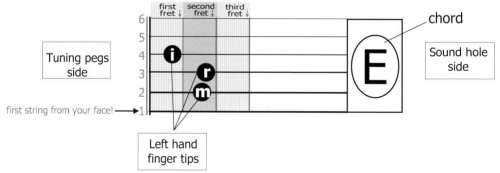

first string from your face!

Speed Tests

Remember; it's not about you comparing yourself to someone else, but about <u>you</u> getting better compared with last week!

I use target times and speed tests in my teaching because it shows students just how well they are progressing. It's not about speed, but it is about finding out how long it takes you to do an exercise as smoothly and cleanly as possible. After a week's practice, you find out that you still play that exercise well, but it takes 20 seconds less time. That's progress!

Target Time and Beginner's Average Time (BAT)

TT: 30-40s:

means that the Target Time you should be aiming at for that step is between 30 and 40 seconds.

BAT:1.00-1.30:

means that the Beginner's Average Time is (usually) between one minute, and one minute thirty seconds.

CHAPTER 1

STEP 1 : E and A

HOW TO PLAY BASIC CHORDS

Let's get started by getting used to reading the chord diagrams of E, then A.

1. Put your index fingertip behind the first fret, fourth string from your face.
2. Put your middle fingertip behind the second fret, second string from your face.
3. Put your ring fingertip behind the second fret, third string from your face.
4. Use your right hand thumb to play all six strings (down-strum FOUR times)

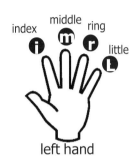

left hand

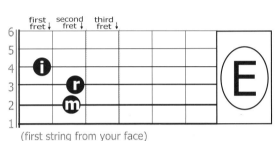

(first string from your face)

Down-strum
X4

5. When you feel quite confident with the E chord, try the A chord.
(down-strum the last five strings with your right hand thumb)

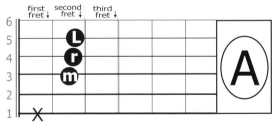

(X means don't play the string!)

Down-strum
X4

toptip

<u>3 ways to a clean
and tidy note</u>

• fingertips only
• pressing down firmly
• right behind the fret!

BASIC CHORDS

STEP 1 : E and A			TT: 20 - 30s		BAT:30 - 40s	
DATE:						
TIME:						

STEP 2 : E, A, B7, E

1. First have a look at the new chord of B7. (It might be easier to decide which fingertips you're going to put down first, and in what order.)
2. Now play the page (starting with E) down-strumming the chords four times each.
3. Practice these chords until you can play them all within the target time (30 - 40 seconds)

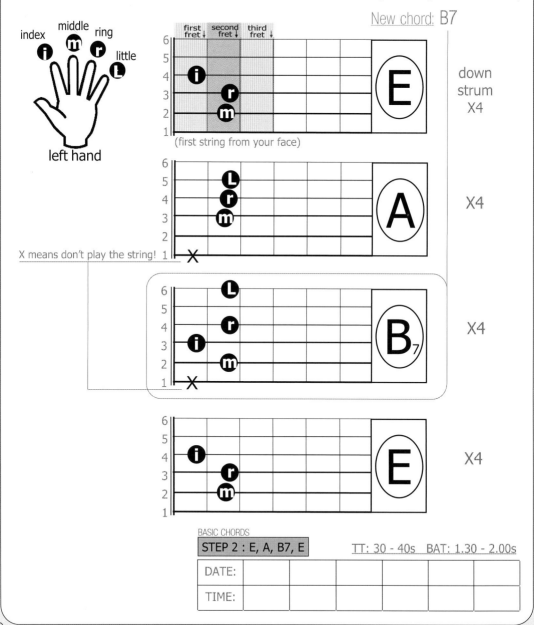

New chord: B7

E down strum X4

A X4

X means don't play the string!

B7 X4

E X4

BASIC CHORDS

STEP 2 : E, A, B7, E   TT: 30 - 40s   BAT: 1.30 - 2.00s

DATE:						
TIME:						

STEP 3 : E, A, B7, E / A, D, E, A

1. First have a look at the new chord of D.

2. Now play the page by down-strumming the chords four times each.

3. Practice these chords until you can play them all within the target time (45 - 55 seconds)

New chord: D

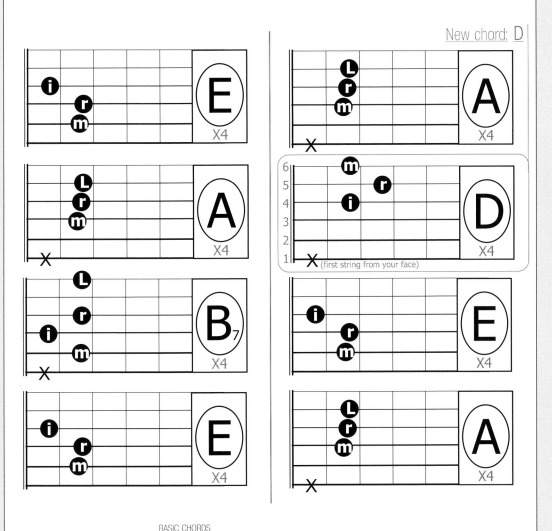

BASIC CHORDS

STEP 3 : E, A, B7, E / A, D, E, A				TT: 45 - 55s BAT: 1.30 - 2.00s			
DATE:							
TIME:							

STEP 4 : 16 Chord block

1. First have a look at the new chords of G and C.

2. Now play the pages by down-strumming the chords <u>four times</u> each.

3. Practice these chords until you can play them all within the target time (45 - 55 seconds)

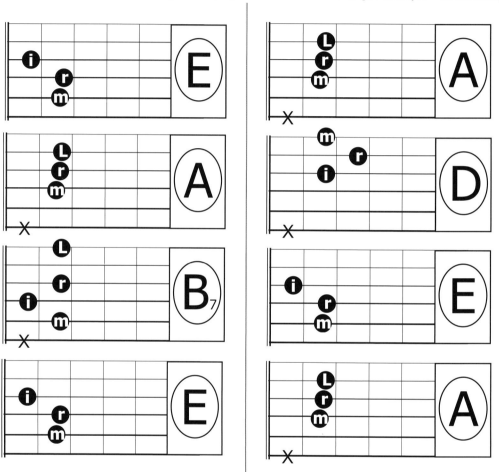

toptip As you play the chords, start to memorise the chord shapes. It will help you to change quicker from one chord to the next.

(Down strum each chord X4)

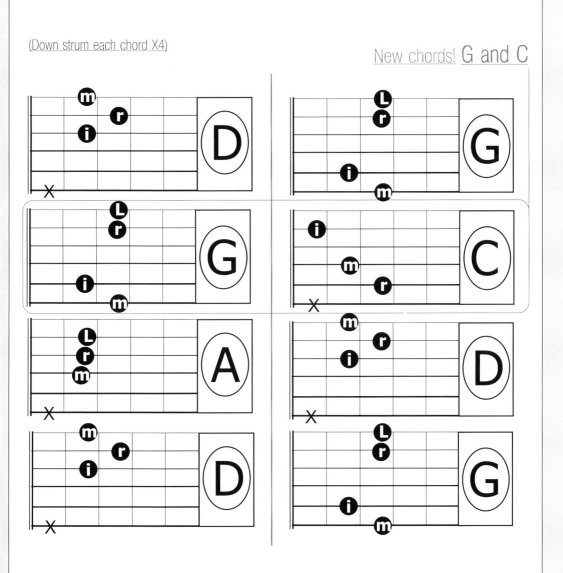

BASIC CHORDS

STEP 4 : 16 Chord block			TT: 45 - 55s	BAT: 1.30 - 2.00s			
DATE:							
TIME:							

STEP 5 : 16 Chord block (strumming)

How to strum:
1. Hold the pick between your right hand thumb and index finger.
2. Make sure the pick is pointing towards you, and the thumb is parallel to the strings.
3. Rest the inside of your elbow on the edge of the guitar body and swing your arm like a pendulum so the pick strums over the sound hole. (DON'T twist the wrist but try and keep your arm/hand nice and straight!)
4. Play E, and strum 1 and 2 and 3 and 4 and.
        REMEMBER: always start with the down stroke - 'ands' are always upstroke.
5. Practice the 16 chord block until you can strum it all within the target time (45 - 55 seconds)

(now play across in rows rather than in columns)

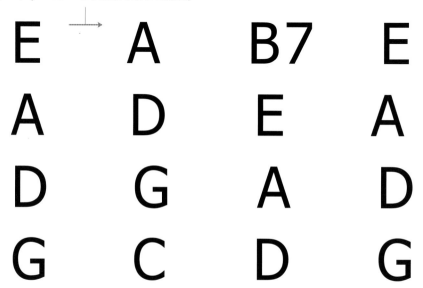

E	A	B7	E
A	D	E	A
D	G	A	D
G	C	D	G

1 2 3 4 = DOWNSTOKE
and's   = UPSTROKE

Arm - keep it straight, and swing from the elbow!

Wrist - keep it straight with the arm!

Thumb - parallel to the strings!

Pick - pointing towards you - hold the pick gently
                        between thumb and index

strumming pattern

1 and 2 and 3 and 4 and

BASIC CHORDS

STEP 4 : 16 Chord block (strumming)	TT: 45 - 55s	BAT: 1.30 - 2.00s

DATE:							
TIME:							

STEP 6 : Advanced strumming patterns

Ideally, this is the page you will want to work from to polish your strumming.
Your knowledge of the (6) chords is such that you remember the particular chord shape very well, and can move your fingers from one chord to the next with less pausing in between.

1. Once you can strum these chords within the target time (45 - 55 seconds) use this page in your regular practice routine.
2. Stick to a slow steady rhythm and go through all the chords using the first strumming pattern.
3. Repeat the 16 chord block using the second strumming pattern, and so on.
4. The process of going through this regularly and consistently will <u>dramatically</u> increase your playing performance.

E →	A	B7	E
A	D	E	A
D	G	A	D
G	C	D	G

<u>Advanced strumming patterns</u>

1)   1 and 2 and 3 and 4 and

2)   1   2 and 3 and 4 and

3)   1   2   3 and 4 and

4)   1 and 2 and   and   and

toptip   All through these strumming patterns the right arm must keep swinging.
The spaces are when you don't allow the pick to touch the strings
as it moves across the sound hole. Just keep that right arm swinging!

STEP 7 : Changing from one chord to another

For this exercise I have chosen E and A, but you can follow this routine for any chord you find difficult to get to quickly.

1. Down-strum once, the chord of E.
2. Down-strum once, the chord of A.
3. Play these chords one after the other for <u>TWO MINUTES</u>.
4. Do the hand exercises;
    Open hands wide for 2 seconds, clench fists for 2 seconds, 20 times.
    Open hands wide for 2 seconds, bend knuckles for 2 seconds (so fingers point to the ground, 20 times)
5. Repeat 1, 2, 3 and 4.

• Repeat above exercise using the strumming pattern instead of one down-strum.

6. Strum the chord of E (1 and 2 and 3 and 4 and)
7. Strum the chord of A (1 and 2 and 3 and 4 and)
8. Strum these chords one after the other for <u>TWO MINUTES</u>.
9. Do the hand exercises.
10. Repeat 6, 7, 8 and 9. (remember; NO GAIN WITHOUT PAIN!)

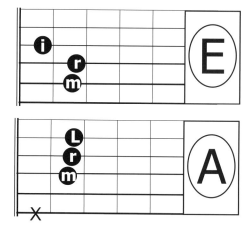

toptip <u>Repeat something enough, and you will master it</u>
Want to get to a chord quickly and cleanly?
Use this routine a couple times a day,
and within a week or two you will perfect it.

CHAPTER 2

HOW TO PLAY BASIC FINGER PICKING

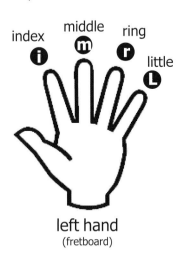

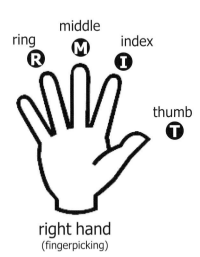

The art of finger picking is a lot more fiddly, but we are going to use the same learning techniques as chord playing.

As we focus on the right hand, you just have to remember that for these basic steps the index, middle, and ring finger are looking after the last 3 strings (4th, 5th, and 6th from your face)

The right hand thumb follows the root note of the chord, (1st, 2nd, or 3rd string from your face) and is clearly marked with a **T**.

Take your time on the next page. Get comfortable with the skill of picking one string at a time.
It will feel awkward at first, but keep at it and it will get smoother!

It's best to begin to learn finger-picking without the left hand
so you can focus on the right hand fingers.

1. Place the left hand on the under body of the guitar where the neck meets the body of the guitar just to steady the instrument as you practice the right hand finger-picking technique.

2. Thumb always follows the root note, and is marked clearly on the chord diagrams below.

3. Index, Middle, and Ring fingers on your right hand always look after the last 3 strings from your face (4th, 5th, and 6th string from your face in that order).

4. Finger-pick the pattern <u>four times</u>.

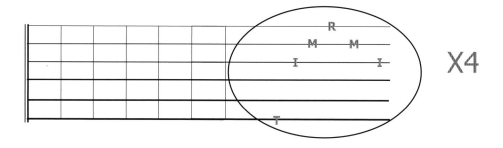

X4

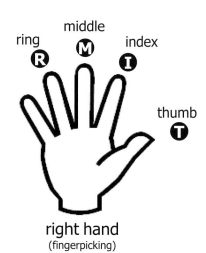

ring middle index

R M I

thumb

T

right hand
(fingerpicking)

toptip Keep the thumb straight
Claw the right hand fingertips
(so they point towards your right shoulder)

STEP 1 : E and A (fp)

1. Finger-pick the chord of E <u>twice</u>.

2. Finger-pick the chord of A <u>twice.</u>

3. Practice the chords until you can finger-pick them both within the target time.

(30 - 40 seconds)

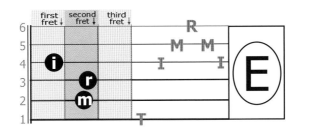

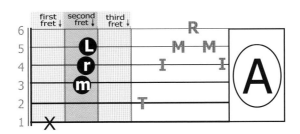

BASIC FINGER-PICKING

STEP 1 : E and A		TT: 30 - 40s	BAT:40 - 50s		
DATE:					
TIME:					

1. Finger-pick the chord of E playing the fp pattern <u>twice.</u>
2. Finger-pick the chord of A playing the fp pattern <u>twice.</u>
3. Finger-pick the chord of B7 playing the fp pattern <u>twice.</u>
4. Finger-pick the chord of E playing the fp pattern <u>twice.</u>
5. Practice the chords until you can finger-pick it all within the target time.

(35 - 45 seconds)

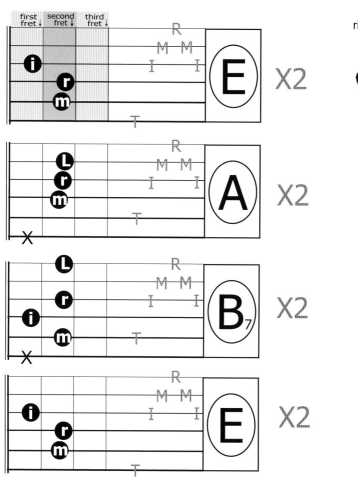

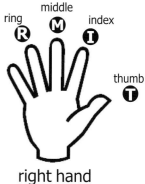

right hand

BASIC FINGER-PICKING

STEP 2 : E, A, B7, E   TT: 35 - 45s   BAT: 1.30 - 2.00s

DATE:						
TIME:						

STEP 3 : E, A, B7, E / A, D, E, A (fp)

1. Finger-pick all 8 chords playing the fp pattern <u>twice on each chord.</u>

T I M R M I (X2)

2. Practice the chords until you can finger-pick it all within the target time.

(45 - 55 seconds)

Remember -

I M R (right hand fingers) always look after the last 3 strings from your face!

(Finger-pick each pattern X2)

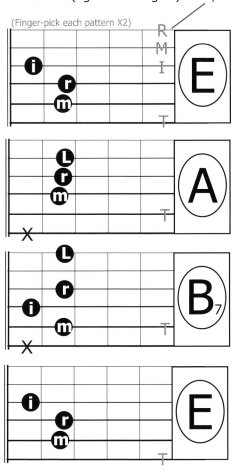

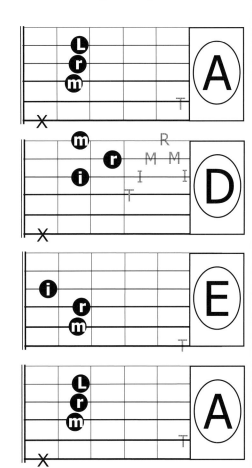

BASIC FINGER-PICKING

STEP 3 : E, A, B7, E / A, D, E, A	TT: 45 - 55s BAT: 1.30 - 2.00s

DATE:							
TIME:							

STEP 4 : 16 chord block (fp)

1. Finger-pick the 16 chord block
(playing the fp pattern <u>twice on each chord</u>)

2. **Practice the chords** until you can finger-pick it all within the target time.
(45 - 55 seconds)

(Right hand thumb root note shown - I M R always look after last 3 strings from your face!)

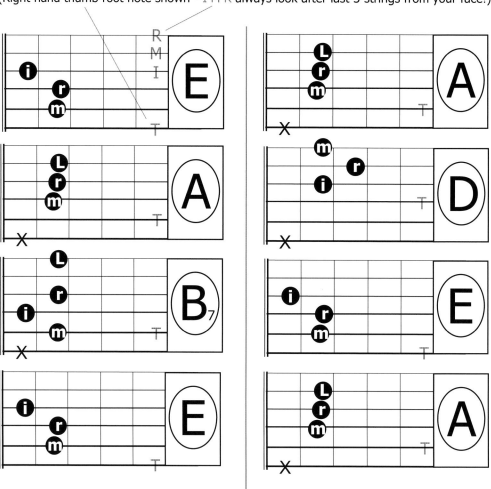

As you are finger-picking one chord, think about the shape of
the next chord and which fingers you will move first.
This will help you to move quickly and (eventually) in time.

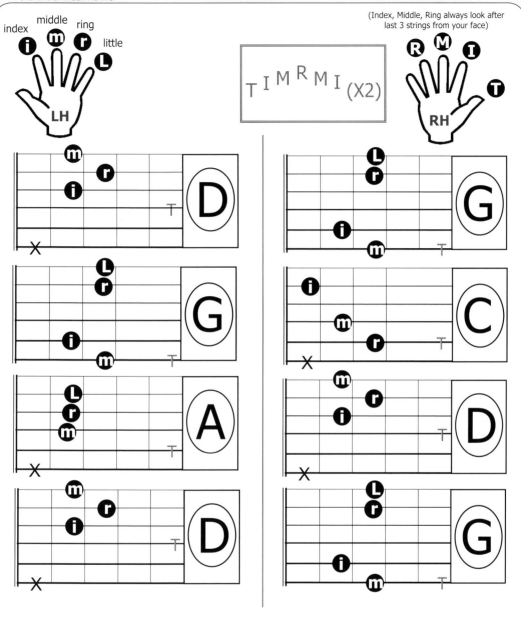

(Index, Middle, Ring always look after last 3 strings from your face)

index   middle   ring

little

LH

RH

T I M R M I (X2)

BASIC FINGER-PICKING

| STEP 4 : 16 Chord block (fp) | TT: 1.00 - 1.10s BAT: 2.00 - 2.30s |

DATE:							
TIME:							

STEP 5 : Advanced finger-picking patterns

1. Once you can finger-pick these chords within the target time (45 - 55 seconds) use this page in your regular practice routine.
2. Stick to a slow steady rhythm and go through all chords using the first finger-picking pattern.
3. Repeat using the second finger-picking pattern, and so on.
4. The process of going through this regularly and consistently (ie everyday for a few weeks!) will dramatically increase your playing performance.

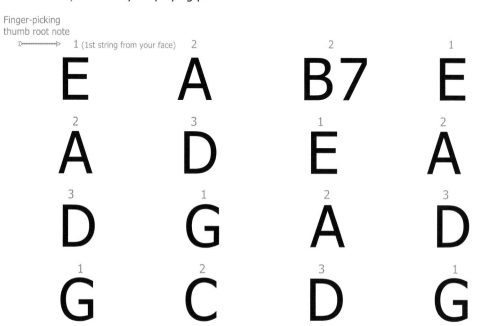

Finger-picking
thumb root note

Advanced finger-picking patterns

1. T ^{I} ^{M} ^{R} $_{M}$ $_{I}$ (X2)   2. T ^{I} $^{M/R}$ $_{I}$ (X2)   3. T ^{I} ^{M} ^{R} (X2)   4. T ^{I} ^{M} ^{R} $_{M}$ $_{I}$ ^{M} $_{I}$

> **toptip**   Finger-picking always feels fiddly and clumsy at the beginning.
> Like everything else the more you do it, the more your fingers will get used to it!

*fp middle and ring together

STEP 5 : 16 Chord block (finger-picking)   TT: 45 - 55s   BAT: 1.30 - 2.00s

DATE:							
TIME:							

STEP 6 : Song - 'Calm Seas'

Finger-pick the song through slowly. Keep a steady rhythm.
Work on changing from one chord to the next without pausing in between.

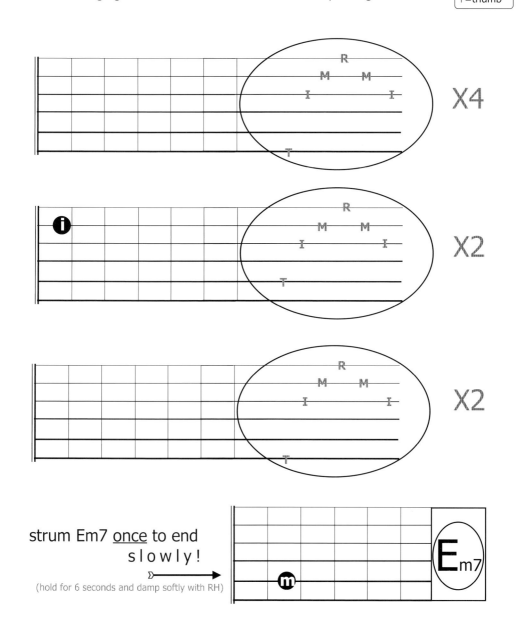

X4

X2

X2

strum Em7 <u>once</u> to end
s l o w l y !

(hold for 6 seconds and damp softly with RH)

Em7

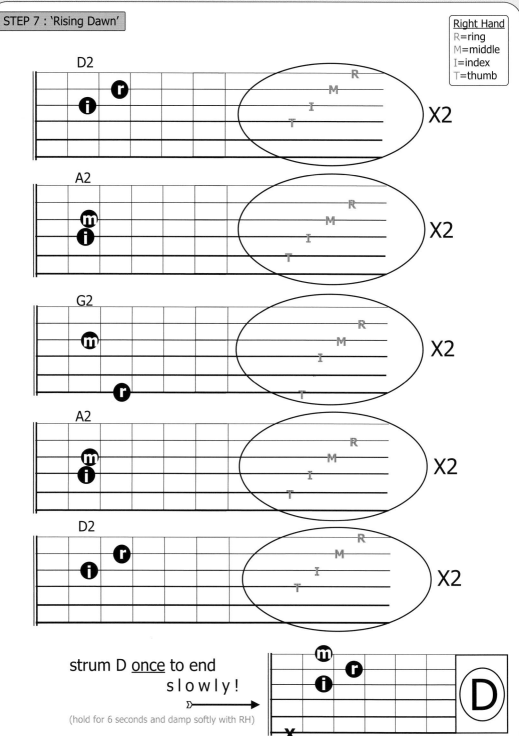

STEP 7 : 'Rising Dawn'

Right Hand
R=ring
M=middle
I=index
T=thumb

D2

X2

A2

X2

G2

X2

A2

X2

D2

X2

strum D once to end
slowly!

(hold for 6 seconds and damp softly with RH)

D

HOW TO PLAY BASIC TAB
(guitar tablature)

<u>The first thing to mention is this;</u>

Don't be scared by the lines, numbers, and letters. It will all become clear in time!
The TAB example below is the song 'Happy Birthday'.
Have a careful look at it, and then read over the 5 TAB basics.
We shall be attempting that song after we have learnt the easiest TAB of all; the FF
scales!

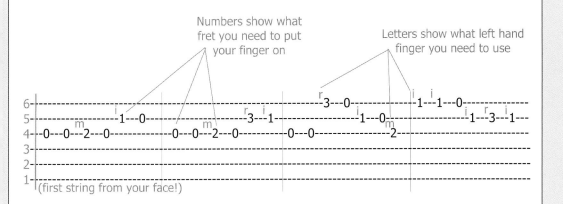

Numbers show what fret you need to put your finger on

Letters show what left hand finger you need to use

(first string from your face!)

The 5 TAB BASICS

1. The 6 lines are the 6 strings of the guitar
2. As in the chord chart, the first string from your face is the thickest string.
3. The numbers on the lines show you what fret to put your fingertips on.
4. The letters by the numbers show you what left hand finger to use.
5. The song (numbers) is played from left to right (follow the roller-coaster!)

Let's get started by learning the easiest TAB of all; The FF scales (Finger to a Fret).

This is not a complicated exercise but don't be fooled into thinking that it's a pointless thing to do - it really is one of the best daily exercises you could do because it hardens your fingertips, strengthens your fingers, and trains you to get around the fret board quickly and cleanly. You want to play lovely sounding notes and chords one day right?...

THIS SIMPLE EXERCISE IS THE SECRET!

However hard and frustrating you might find it at the beginning, prepare to give it two weeks. Battle through for this amount of time and you will be surprised at how far you have come!

● **1. Start the exercise** by placing the left hand thumb behind the 4th fret (half way down behind the neck), and push your wrist forward so that your fingers give the neck plenty of space to breathe.

● **2. Place index finger** on the first string, third fret.
With right hand thumb on the first string (over the sound hole), pluck down once.

● **3. Keeping your index finger** down, now place middle finger on fret 4 (same string)
With right hand thumb on the first string, pluck down once.

● **4. Keeping your middle finger** down, now place ring finger on fret 5 (same string)
With right hand thumb on the first string, pluck down once.

● **5. Keeping your ring finger down,** now place little finger on fret 6
(same string) With right hand thumb on the first string, pluck down once.

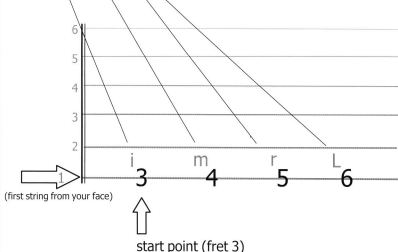

(first string from your face)

start point (fret 3)

STEP 1 : FF scales (basic level)

This first step takes you down from the first string (from your face) to the last string, playing all 4 notes on frets 3, 4, 5, and 6.

1. Practice these FF scales (fret 3 down) until you can play it within the target time.

(45 - 55 seconds)

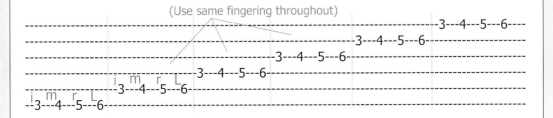

(Use same fingering throughout)

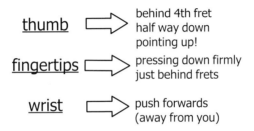

thumb ⇒ behind 4th fret
half way down
pointing up!

fingertips ⇒ pressing down firmly
just behind frets

wrist ⇒ push forwards
(away from you)

toptip 3 ways to a clean and tidy note...
1. fingertips only...
2. pressing down firmly...
3. right behind the frets !

BASIC TAB

STEP 1 : FF scales (fret 3 down)	TT: 45 - 55s BAT: 1.30 - 2.00s						
DATE:							
TIME:							

STEP 2 : FF scales (medium level)

This second step takes you down from the first string (from your face) to the last string <u>and back to the first string,</u> playing all 4 notes on frets 3, 4, 5, and 6.

1. Practice these FF scales (fret 3 down and back) until you can play it within the target time (45 - 55 seconds)

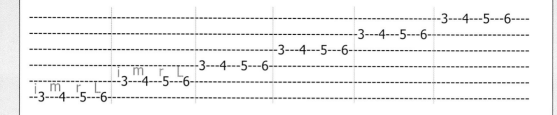

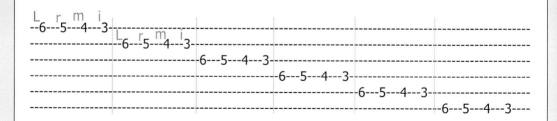

toptip   FF scales are one of the most important exercises you can do!
They harden your fingertips, strengthen your fingers, and speed up your movement around the fretboard.

BASIC TAB

STEP 2 : FF scales (fret 3 down/back)							
DATE:							
TIME:							

TT: 45 - 55s   BAT: 1.30 - 2.00s

STEP 3 : Basic TAB songs

This third step introduces 3 simple TAB songs.

1. Go over each one slowly to begin with. Make sure you are using the right fingering!
As you practice each one over and over, you will slowly see improvements in the speed test.

SONG: Happy Birthday

Target Time: 20-30s

DATE:						
TIME:						

```
                                                              r         i  i
6--------------------------------------------------------3---0-----------1---1--0------------------
5------------------1---0---------------------3---1----------------1--0---------------1--r3---i1---
      m                                  m                    i     m                1--3---1---
4---0---0---2---0---------------0---0---2---0---------0---0------------------2----------------------
3-------------------------------------------------------------------------------------------------
2-------------------------------------------------------------------------------------------------
1-------------------------------------------------------------------------------------------------
  (first string from your face!)
```

SONG: O When the Saints

Target Time: 20-30s

DATE:						
TIME:						

```
           i          i            i                              i   i           i
6--------0--2-------0--2--------0--2-------------------------2---2---0--------0--2-------------
5--0--4-------0--4-------0--4--------4--0--4--2--4--4---2--0--4------------4--4--------4--0-2--0-
      r        r       r            r     r  r   r    i     r                 r         r
4---------------------------------------------------------------------------------------------
3---------------------------------------------------------------------------------------------
2---------------------------------------------------------------------------------------------
1---------------------------------------------------------------------------------------------
  (first string from your face!)
```

SONG: Yankee Doodle

Target Time: 20-30s

DATE:						
TIME:						

```
          i   i                    i                          i  m  i
6--m--m---0--2---2--0--------m--m---0--2-------m--m------0--2--3--2--0--------------------------
5--3--3-------3-------------------3--3-------3--2-------3--3-----------3----2----0--2--3--3------
      m        m        i      m        m         i    m        m       i       i  m  m
4--------------------2----------------------2---------------------------2----------------------
3---------------------------------------------------------------------------------------------
2---------------------------------------------------------------------------------------------
1---------------------------------------------------------------------------------------------
```

STEP 4 : 12 Bar Blues (in E)

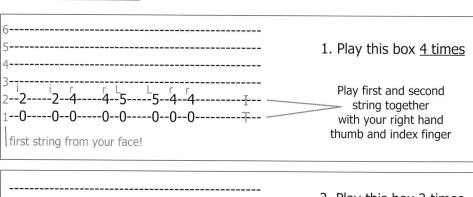

```
6-----------------------------------------------
5-----------------------------------------------
4-----------------------------------------------
3-------------------------------------------
2--2-----2--4-----4--5-----5--4--4---------+--
1--0-----0--0-----0--0-----0--0--0---------+--
```
| first string from your face!

1. Play this box 4 times

Play first and second
string together
with your right hand
thumb and index finger

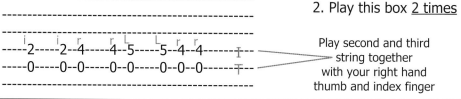

```
-----------------------------------------------
-----------------------------------------------
-----------------------------------------------
-----2-----2--4-----4--5-----5--4--4------+--
-----0-----0--0-----0--0-----0--0--0------+--
-----------------------------------------------
```

2. Play this box 2 times

Play second and third
string together
with your right hand
thumb and index finger

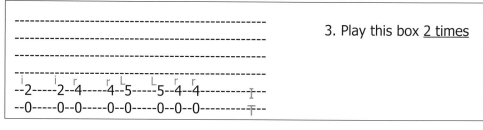

```
-----------------------------------------------
-----------------------------------------------
-----------------------------------------------
-----------------------------------------------
--2-----2--4-----4--5-----5--4--4---------+--
--0-----0--0-----0--0-----0--0--0---------+--
```

3. Play this box 2 times

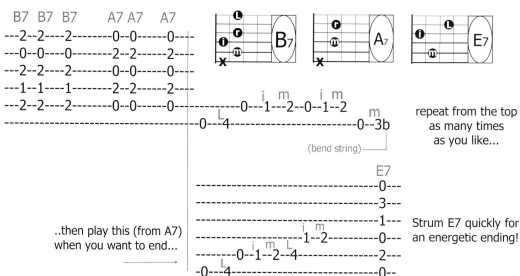

```
   B7  B7  B7      A7 A7   A7
---2--2----2--------0--0------0---
---0--0----0--------2--2------2---
---2--2----2--------0--0------0---
---1--1----1--------2--2------2---
---2--2----2--------0--0------0---
----------------------------------
```

```
                           i  m     i  m
-------------------0---1---2--0--1--2        m
------------0--4-----------------------0--3b
```
(bend string)

repeat from the top
as many times
as you like...

..then play this (from A7)
when you want to end...

```
                                    E7
-------------------------------0---
-------------------------------3---
-------------------------1---1---
-----------------1--2----------0---
--------0--1--2--4-------------2---
-0---4------------------------0--
```
i m L / i m

Strum E7 quickly for
an energetic ending!

STEP 5 : Blues scale (in E)

This is a basic blues scale (in E).

Play this over and over until it sounds smooth.

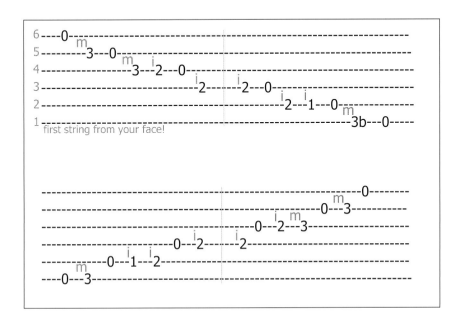

Do you know someone else who plays guitar?
- ask them to play STEP 4, while you play STEP 5!

Remember, you don't have to play the blues scale in this order - play the
notes in different ways and have fun making up your own solo!

BASIC TAB

STEP 5 : Blues scale (in E)		Target Time: 20-30s			
DATE:					
TIME:					

STEP 6 : Major scale/Blues scale

These basic scales are important to learn off by heart. Being able to play them quickly and smoothly will be the key to your first important steps in playing riffs and lead solos.

They have been written using finger names and not TAB because they can be played using the same pattern, starting at any fret on the fret board.

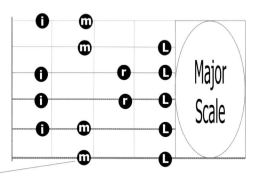

Start point

STEP 6 : Major Scale (start point fret 3, 4, 5, 4, 3)						
DATE:						
TIME:						

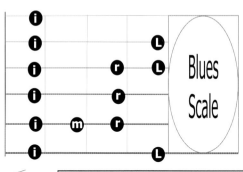

Start point

STEP 6 : Blues Scale (start point fret 3, 4, 5, 4, 3)						
DATE:						
TIME:						

The blues scale (based around the pentatonic scale) is one of the most commonly used scales as a basis for many great riffs and lead solos. The notes can be played in either ascending or descending order, and you can combine them in any way that gives you the right sound.
Some notes can be left out, and others can be added.
The start point note gives you the key you are playing in, and providing someone else is playing a song in the same key, you will be heading in the right direction!

There are no strict rules to improvising lead solos; just listen for what sounds good, and experiment!

STEP 7 : FF scales (advanced level)

This step 7 is simply STEP 2 played 5 times on different fret starting points.

1. Play fret 3 down and back up.

2. Slide index up to the 4th fret * (thumb behind the 5th), and go down and back.
3. Slide index up to the 5th fret (thumb behind the 6th), and go down and back.
4. Slide index down to the 4th fret (thumb behind the 5th), and go down and back.
5. Slide index down to the 3rd fret (thumb behind the 4th), and go down and back.

* example of TAB for the FF scales starting at fret 4

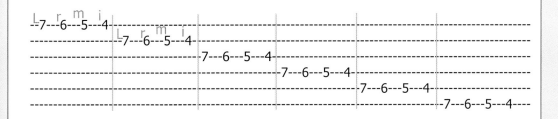

BASIC TAB

STEP 7 : FF scales (fret 3, 4, 5, 4, 3)		TT: 50 - 60s BAT: 3.00 - 3.30s					
DATE:							
TIME:							

Well done, you've made it this far!
You have covered the most important foundations of the book, and are ready to put what you have learnt into context!

TO BECOME A GREAT GUITARIST YOU NEED..

SONGS and PERFORMANCE

PRACTICE and EXERCISES

THIS...........AND.........THAT!

Too much of this won't get you far!
You will never learn the skills to become a better guitarist!
Do some proper practice and exercises..
- your songs will sound so much better!

Too much of this is boring.
You need to work at polishing your performance.
Learn some new songs..
That's what learning the guitar is all about!

final toptips! You will achieve much better results by practicing little and often.
Try 10-15 minutes 4/5 times a week. Spend this time on <u>real</u> practice (repetition of FF scales and 16 chord block) as opposed to fake practice (going over your favourite songs and riffs, and not really pushing the pain barrier with your fingers!) Let the songs and riffs be the reward for working hard on your exercises, your playing will sound so much better - **work hard, play hard!**

BITE-SIZE TAB AND SONG CHORD CHARTS

CHAPTER 4

BITZ OF BITE-SIZE TAB AND SONG CHORD CHARTS

'James Bond 007' (Norman and Barry)

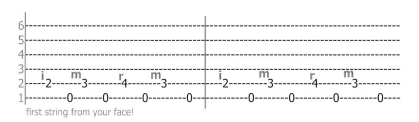

first string from your face!

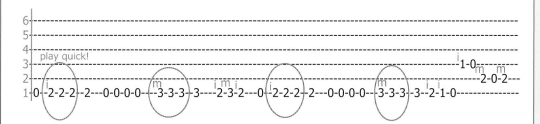

play quick!

'The Simpsons' (Elfman)

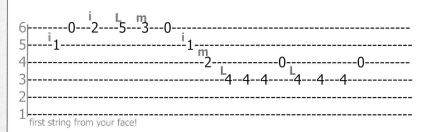

first string from your face!

'Can't Stop' (Red Hot Chili Peppers)

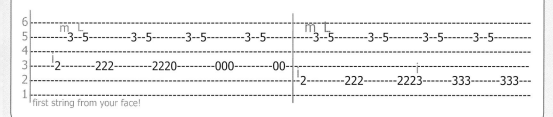

first string from your face!

'Zephyr Song' (Red Hot Chili Peppers)

(play these two notes together)

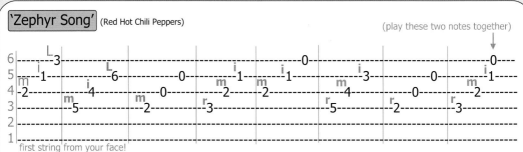

first string from your face!

'By the Way' (Red Hot Chili Peppers)

(play X8)

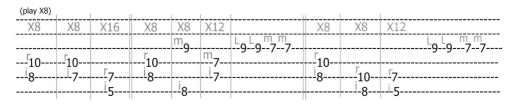

'Smoke on the Water' (Deep Purple)

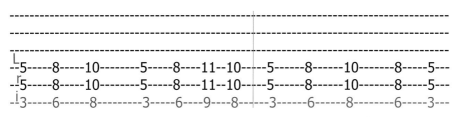

(an easier version could be played just using the index finger on the first string from your face)

'Sunshine' (Clapton)

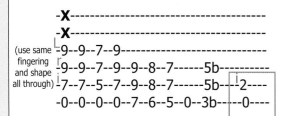

1 - all
2 - all except box
3 - all
4 - all except box

'We will rock you' (Queen)

```
-------------------------------------------
-------------------------------------------
-------------------------------------------
--ⁱ5--ⁱ4--ⁱ2--ⁱ0--ⁱ2-2--ⁱ-2-2----  X4
-------------------------------------------
--------------------0-0----0-0----
```

'5 Colours in her hair' (McFly)

```
--------------------------------------------------------------------------------
--------------------------------------------------------------------------------
--------------------------------------------------------------------------------
----------------0-ⁱ3-4-5-5-3-5-3----------------0-ⁱ3-4-5-5-3-5-3------------------------
       ⁱ_mⁱ_rⁱ_r                        ʳ_mⁱ_3-ⁱ1-ⁱ3              ʳ_mⁱ_ⁱ  ⁱ_ⁱ_m ʳ
      --1-2-3-1-3----------------------5--4-3-1-1-3------------------------5-4-3-1-3--1-3-4-5--(x16!)
  ʳ_3ⁱ_1ʳ_3
--3-1-3-3---------------------------------------------------------------------------
```

'Mission Impossible theme' (Shifrin)

```
                                          ᴸ_6--ⁱ3------ᴸ_6--ⁱ3-----ᴸ_6--ⁱ3-------------
--------------------------------------------ⁱ3-----------ⁱ2------------ⁱ1--------------
------------------------------------------------------------------------ⁱ3--ʳ5---------
        ⁱ_1--ʳ_3
--ʳ_3ʳ_3--------ʳ_3ʳ_3---ⁱ_1ᵐ_2   X2
```

'Come as you are' (Nirvana)

```
-----------------------------------------------------
-----------------------------------------------------
-----------------------------------------------------
-----------------------------------------------ᵐ---------ᵐ----------
----------ⁱ_mᵐ_0---0------------m_m_i----------2---------2---   Repeat!
---0--1--2----2--------2--2--1--0-----0-0--------
```

'Wish you a Merry Christmas'

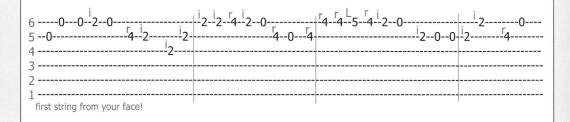

first string from your face!

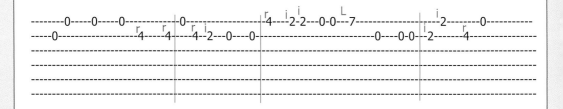

'Jingle Bells'

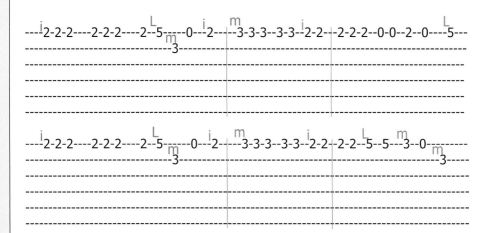

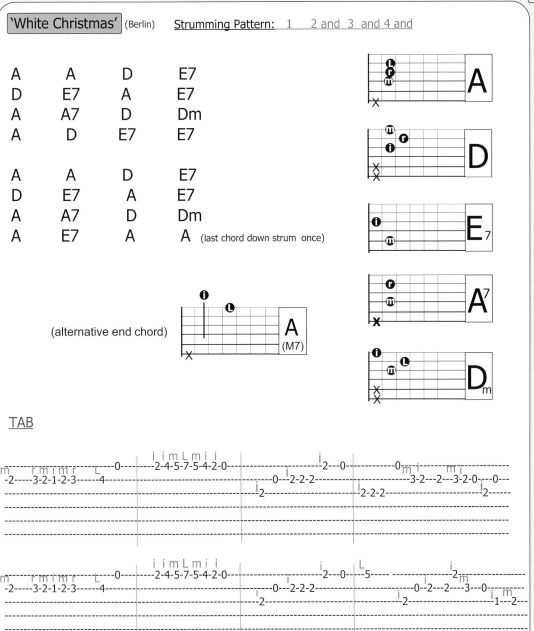

'White Christmas' (Berlin)   Strumming Pattern: 1   2 and 3 and 4 and

A	A	D	E7
D	E7	A	E7
A	A7	D	Dm
A	D	E7	E7

A	A	D	E7
D	E7	A	E7
A	A7	D	Dm
A	E7	A	A (last chord down strum once)

(alternative end chord)   A (M7)

TAB

'Soft Steps' (Finger picking duet)

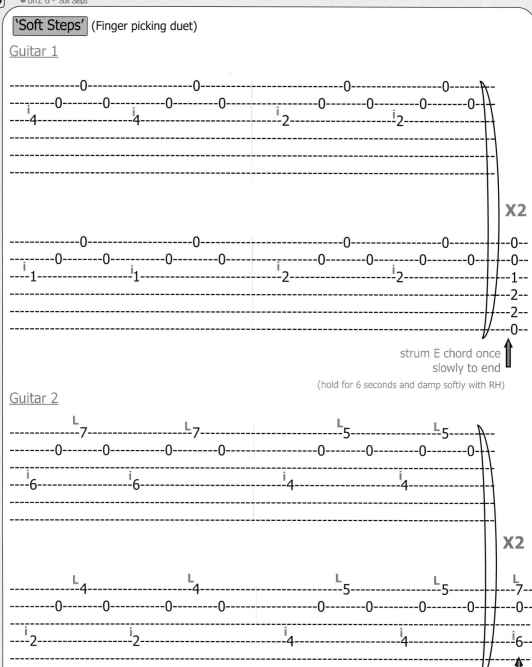

'Stairway' (Led Zeppelin)

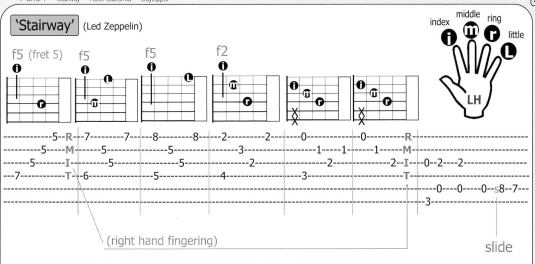

'Hotel California' (The Eagles)

1   2   3 and 4 and   and   and 7 and 8 and

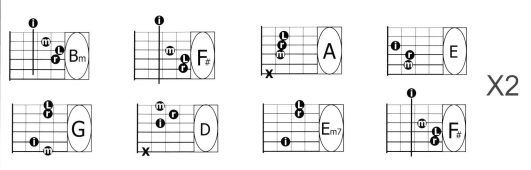

X2

Chorus:
G   D   Em7   Bm
G   D   Em7   F#

'Daytripper' (The Beatles)

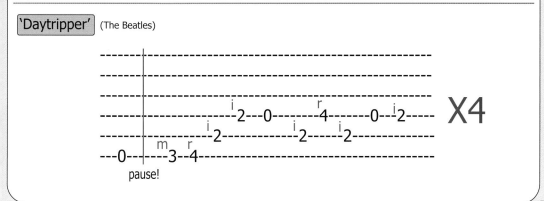

X4

'The Flintstones' (Curtin, Barbera, and Hanna)

Remember the right fingering!!
i m r l
Frets 5 6 7 8

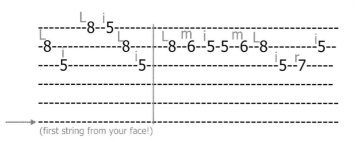

(first string from your face!)

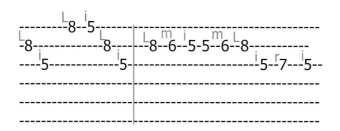

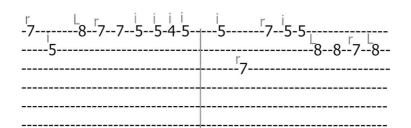

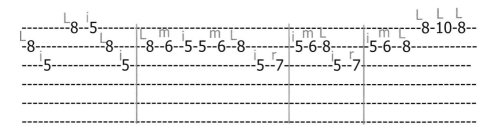

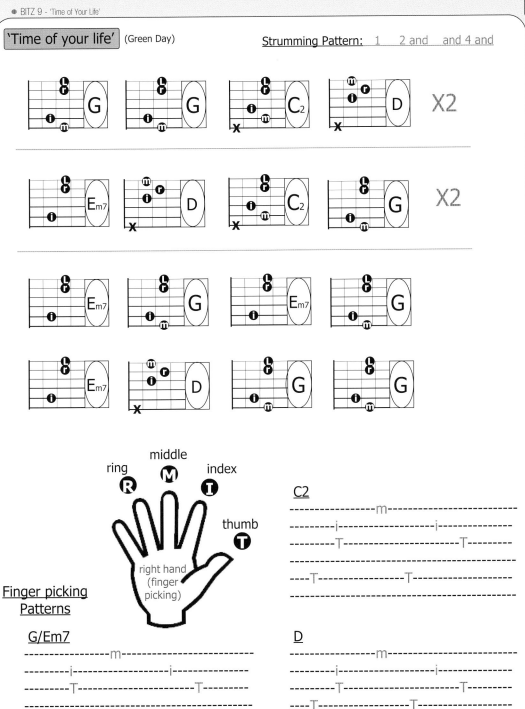

'Hallelujah' (theme from 'Shrek' - Leonard Cohen)

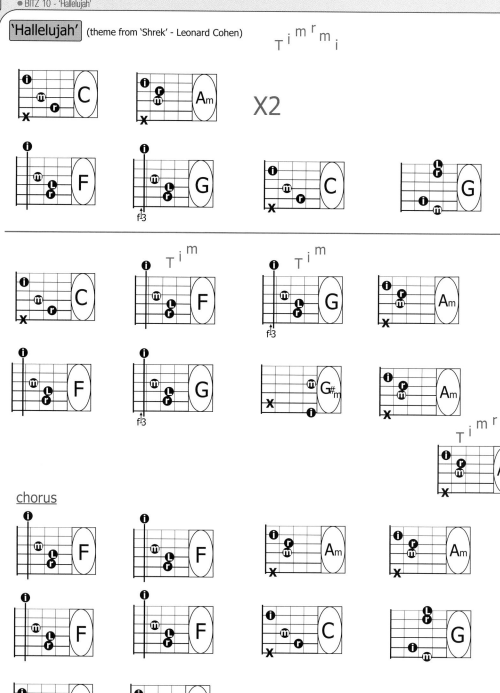

chorus

(down strum C once to end)

'September' (Green Day)

```
---------------------------------------------------------------------------------------------------
---------i----------i-----|---------------i----------i-----|---------r----------r-----|------r----------r-----
------3--------3-----|         |------3--------3-----|------3--------3--|------3--------3--
------0--------0-----|X4   |------0--------0--|-m---0-------0--|--i--0-------0--|---0-------0--
---r5---------r5-----|         |--r5---------r5--|--4---------m4--|-2--------i2--|--0--------0--
---------------------------|         |--------------------|--------------------|-------------------
---------------------------|         |--------------------|--------------------|-------------------
```

```
---------------------------------------------------------------------------------------------------
---------r----------r-----|---------L----------L-----|---------r----------r-----|------r----------r-----
------3--------3-----|------4--------4--|------3--------3--|------3--------3--
------0--------0-----|------0--------0--|------0--------0--|------0--------0--
-m-3--------m3-----|--m-3--------m3--|--------------------|-------------------
---------------------------|---------------------------|--m-3--------m3--|-m-3-------m3--
```

'Unintended' (Muse)

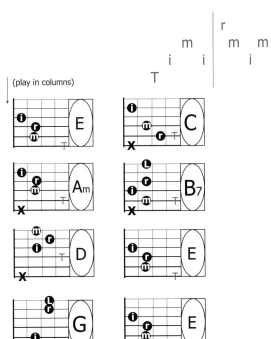

(play in columns)

E   C

Am   B₇

D   E

G   E

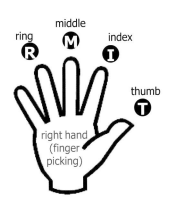

middle
ring   M   index
R   I

thumb
T

right hand
(finger
picking)

'He's got the whole world' (Trad)

1   2 and 3 and 4 and
(see a chord - strum the pattern!)

        E   E
He's got the whole world in His hands,
        B7   E
He's got the whole world in His hands,
        E   E
He's got the whole world in His hands.
        B7   E
He's got the whole world in His hands.

2. He's got the wind and the rain in His hands, (X3)
He's got the whole world in His hands.

3. He's got the tiny little baby in His hands, (X3)
He's got the whole world in His hands.

'Happy Birthday' (strumming)

(Play G down stroke once to begin)

      1 2 and 3 and   1 2 and 3 and
       G   D
Happy Birthday to you

      1 2 and 3 and   1 2 and 3 and
       D   G
Happy Birthday to you

     1 2 and 3 and   1   1
     G   C2 C2 (pause!..)
Happy Birthday dear doo da

  1   1   1   1   1
  C2   G   G D G
Happy Birthday to you

'Swing Low' (Trad)

1   2 and 3 and 4 and

(see a chord - strum the pattern!)

```
        E   E       A   E
Swing low,  sweet chariot,
  E           E       B7   B7
Comin' for to carry me home;
       E  E7      A    E
Swing low, sweet chariot,
  E           B7      E      E
Comin' for to carry me home.
```

```
     E          E          A       E
Well I looked over Jordan, and what did I see,
  E           E       B7    B7
Comin' for to carry me home;
   E      E7    A        E
A band of angels coming after me,
  E           B7      E     E
Comin' for to carry me home.
```

'Comin' round the mountain' (Trad)

1   2 and 3 and 4 and

(see a chord - strum the pattern!)

```
       E                E             E    E
She'll be comin' round the mountain when she comes
       E                E             B7   B7
She'll be comin' round the mountain when she comes
       E              E7
She'll be comin' round the mountain
       A             A
She'll be comin' round the mountain
  E              B7            E    E
comin' round the mountain when she comes
```

2. She'll be drivin' six white horses when she comes.....

3. Oh, we'll all go out to meet her when she comes.....

'Oh when the saints' (Trad)

1   2 and 3 and 4 and

(see a chord - strum the pattern!)

```
          E   E              E    E
Oh when the saints    go marching in
          E     E       B7   B7
Oh when the saints go marching in,
     E  E7      A      A
I wanna be in that number,
          E      B7      E   E
Oh when the saints go marching in
```

'My Bonnie' (Trad)

1   2 and 3 and   (note new $\frac{3}{4}$ strumming pattern)

(see a chord - strum the pattern!)

```
    E         A      E     E
My Bonnie lies over the ocean,
    E         E      B7    B7
My Bonnie lies over the sea,
    E         A      E     E
My Bonnie lies over the ocean,
     A              B7     E    E
Oh bring back my Bonnie to me.
```

chorus
```
  E    E    A   A
Bring back, bring back,
     B7          B7      E     E
Oh bring back my Bonnie to me, to me,
  E    E    A   A
Bring back, bring back,
     B7          B7      E     E
Oh bring back my Bonnie to me.
```

'Head, Shoulders....' (Trad)

1   2 and 3 and 4 and
(see a chord - strum the pattern!)

D   D   D   D
Head, shoulders, knees and toes, knees and toes.
D   D   A   A
Head, shoulders, knees and toes, knees and toes.
     D   D7   G   G
And eyes and ears, and a mouth and a nose.
  A   A   D   D
Head, shoulders, knees and toes, knees and toes.

(Chord diagrams: D, A, D7, G)

'Amazing Grace' (Newton)

1   2 and 3 and
(see a chord - strum the pattern!)

    E   E7   A   E
Amazing grace how sweet the sound
     E   E   B7   B7
That saved a wretch like me
    E   E7   A   E
I once was lost but now am found
      E   B7   A   E
Was blind but now I see

(Chord diagrams: E, E7, A, B7)

TAB
```
-----0---0--r-i-2--0---r--i-2---0----------------0---0--r-i-2--0--r---i--i--L-
                 4           4                                 4        2   4   7--
--0-----------------------------------2-0---0------------------------------------
--------------------------------------------------------------------------------
--------------------------------------------------------------------------------
--------------------------------------------------------------------------------
--------------------------------------------------------------------------------
```

```
--i-L-L----i--i----r--i------------------0---r-i------0---r--i-----0---
  4  7--7----4--2---0---4------2----0-------4--2----------4----2----
------------------------------2--0---0-------------------------------
--------------------------------------------------------------------
--------------------------------------------------------------------
--------------------------------------------------------------------
--------------------------------------------------------------------
```

'Friends' theme ('Ill be there' - Rembrandts)

1   2 and 3 and 4 and

(see a chord - strum the pattern!)

f↑4 (fret 4)

(This chord
down strum
once to end)

'Street Spirit' (Radiohead)

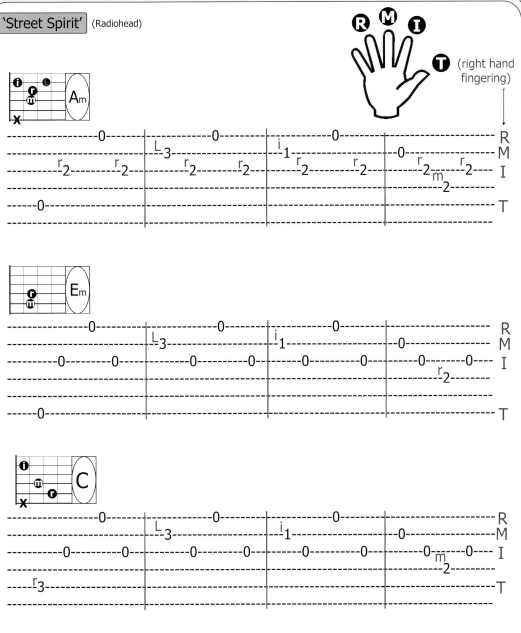

Song order: Am X4   Em X2   Am X2   C   Em   Am X2

slow down
then down strum Am
once to end

'Minuet in G' (Bach)

<u>right hand finger picking</u>
On this song the thumb looks after the first 3 strings from you face, while the index, middle and ring finger look after the last strings from your face.

index middle ring little
i m r L

left hand
finger picking
(fretboard)

R M I
T

```
------------------------------------------------|------------0---------------0---2---3------------------------
L-3------------------------0---i1-----L-3--------|------------i-1--L-3---------------------------------------------
----------0---2-----------------------0-------0--|--------------------------------------0--------0-------------
-------------------------------------------------|--------------------------------------------------------------
r-3-------------0----------m-2------------------|--------r-3----------------------------i-2--------------------
                                                 |
 1    2 + 3  +   1   2   3 |  1    2 + 3  + |  1    2    3
* 3/4 Time signature (3 beats in a bar)
```

```
i-1------r-3--i1---0----------0------i1---0-----|------------------0--------------------------------------------
                   m-2------------------------m-2---0---      m-2-------------0---i-2------------------------
                                            m-4              0---                 0-----0---m-i-2--0---
--0--------------------------------------------r-5------i-2----------------------3--
                          r-3-                              r-3-
 1    2 + 3  +   1   2 + 3  + |  1    2 + 3  + 1 |  2  + 3  +
```

```
----------------------------------------------- |------------0---------------0---2---L-3------------------------
L-3------------------------0---i1-----L-3--------|------------i-1--L-3--------------------------------------------
----------0---2-----------------------0-------0--|--------------------------------------0-------0-------------
i-2------------------------0----------m-2--------|--------r-3----------------------i-2----m-3--i-2--0-----------
                          r-3-           r-3-                                                     m-3
 1    2 + 3  +   1   2   3 |  1    2 + 3  + |  1    2 + 3  +
```

```
i-1------r-3--i1---0----------0------i1--0-------|------------------0-------------------------------------------
                   m-2------------------m-2---0---  m-2------------m-2--0------------0---------------------
                                             i-2------r-3          0-------0--r-4--------------------
--0------------------------------------------------------                       i-3
        i-2-----r-3-                                          
 1    2 + 3  + | 1    2 + 3  + |  1    2 + 3  + |  1    2    3
```

* this time line is useful for students already familiar with the classical time signature of 3/4 (3 beats in a bar)
It will help with the general time keeping, showing what notes are played on which beats of the bar.

I hope this book has helped and inspired you to develop in your guitar playing. It has always been my aim to make this most beautiful skill accessible and as easy to understand as possible. For everyone.

If this book encourages you, and gives you a little more confidence that you can do great things on the guitar - then it has been worthwhile. Often, it is only when you believe that even <u>you yourself</u> can achieve something, that inspiration comes. It's that inspiration that gives you the determination and motivation to practice and 'make perfect'.

If Jesus himself said 'anything is possible if a person believes' (The Bible: Mark 9 v23) then there must be something powerful that takes place in our human condition the very moment we decide to 'have faith' about something. Fear of failure and doubt in your performance will always slow you down. In your quest to become as good as you can be, you will always be tempted to think: 'I'm not getting any better' - 'I'm not half as good as that person' - 'It's just too hard'. But you must try and always respond positively by reminding yourself of the truth; 'little by little, step by step, it's the bite size practice <u>that you *can* do</u> every day or two that will make perfect over time'.

Remember, this is not will power, it's a principle of life, so it has to work.
You <u>will</u> get better! You <u>will</u> progress!

There will be questions that I have not answered in this book. I have tried to make the process as simple and easy to understand, so invariably have had to leave out information that might confuse, or maybe more appropriate to learn at a later stage. Most can be answered by more experienced players that you know, or your helpful and friendly local guitar shop!

If you have any questions, quibbles, or queries relating to anything in this book,
please feel free to email me direct; andy@guitarsteps.com

GO FOR IT!

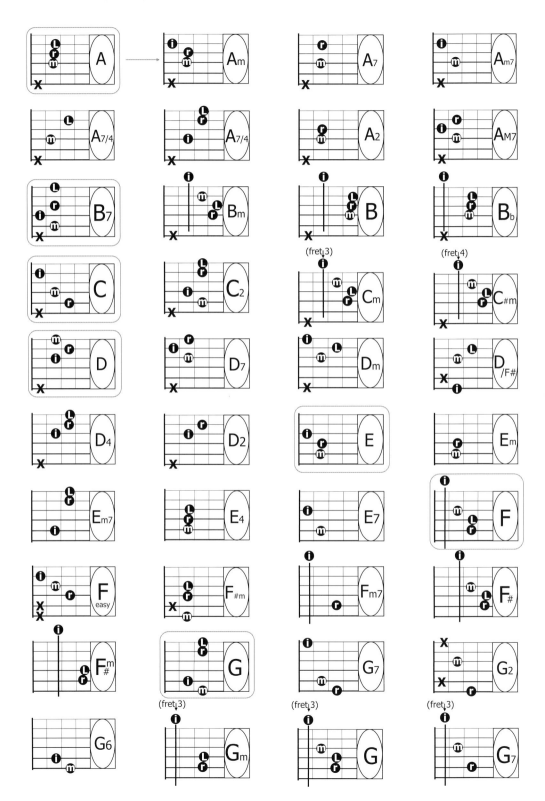